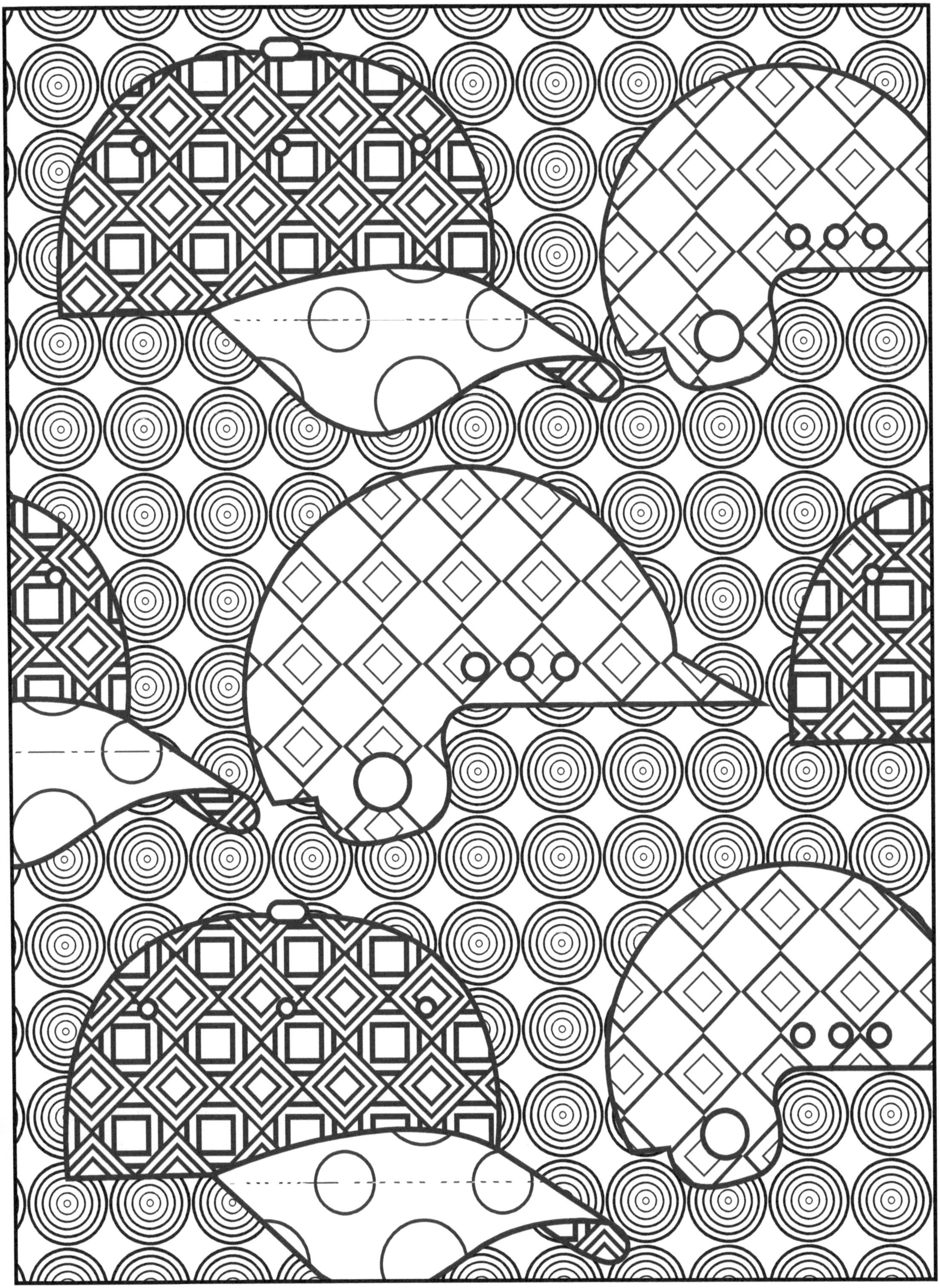

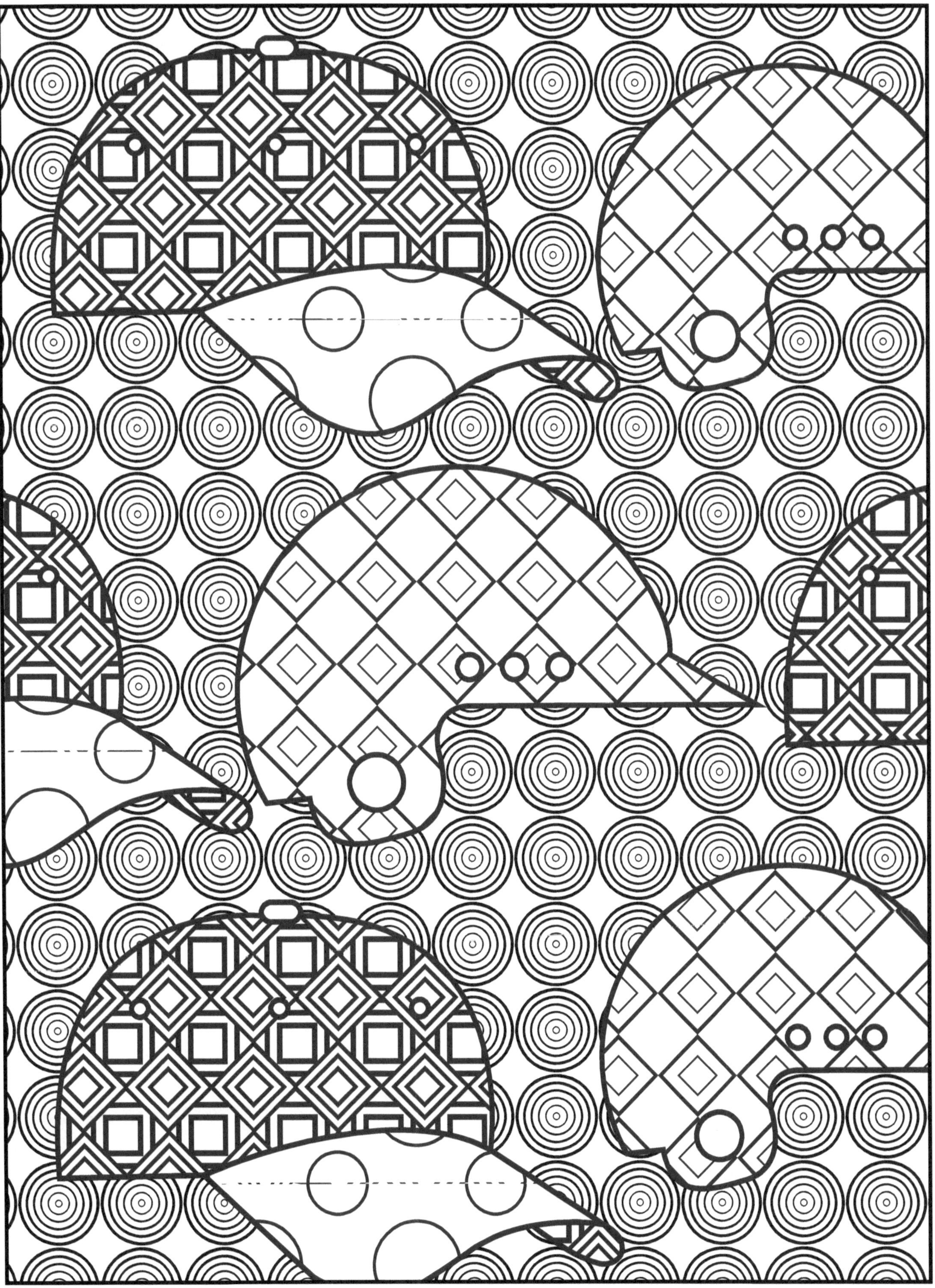

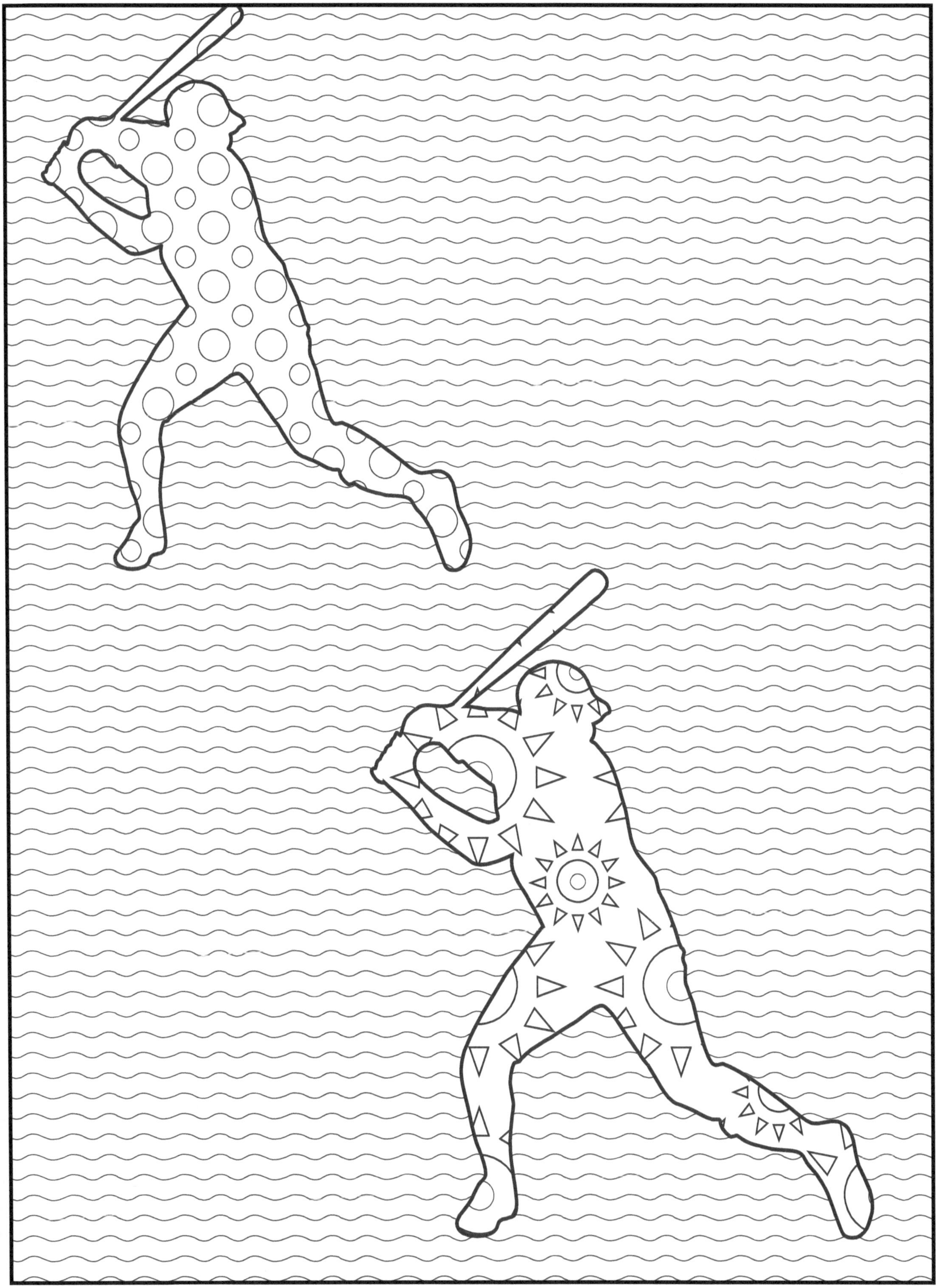

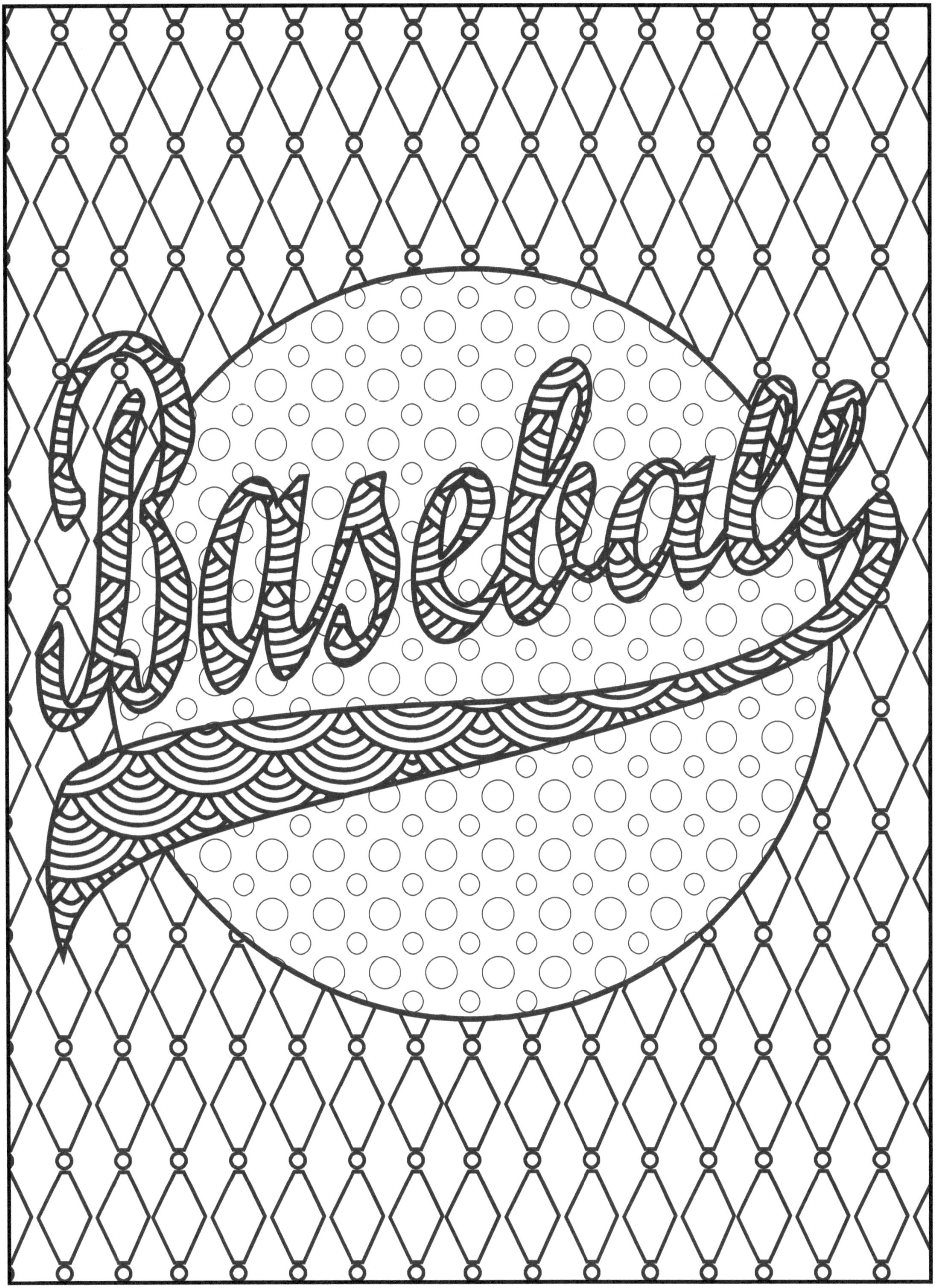
Baseball

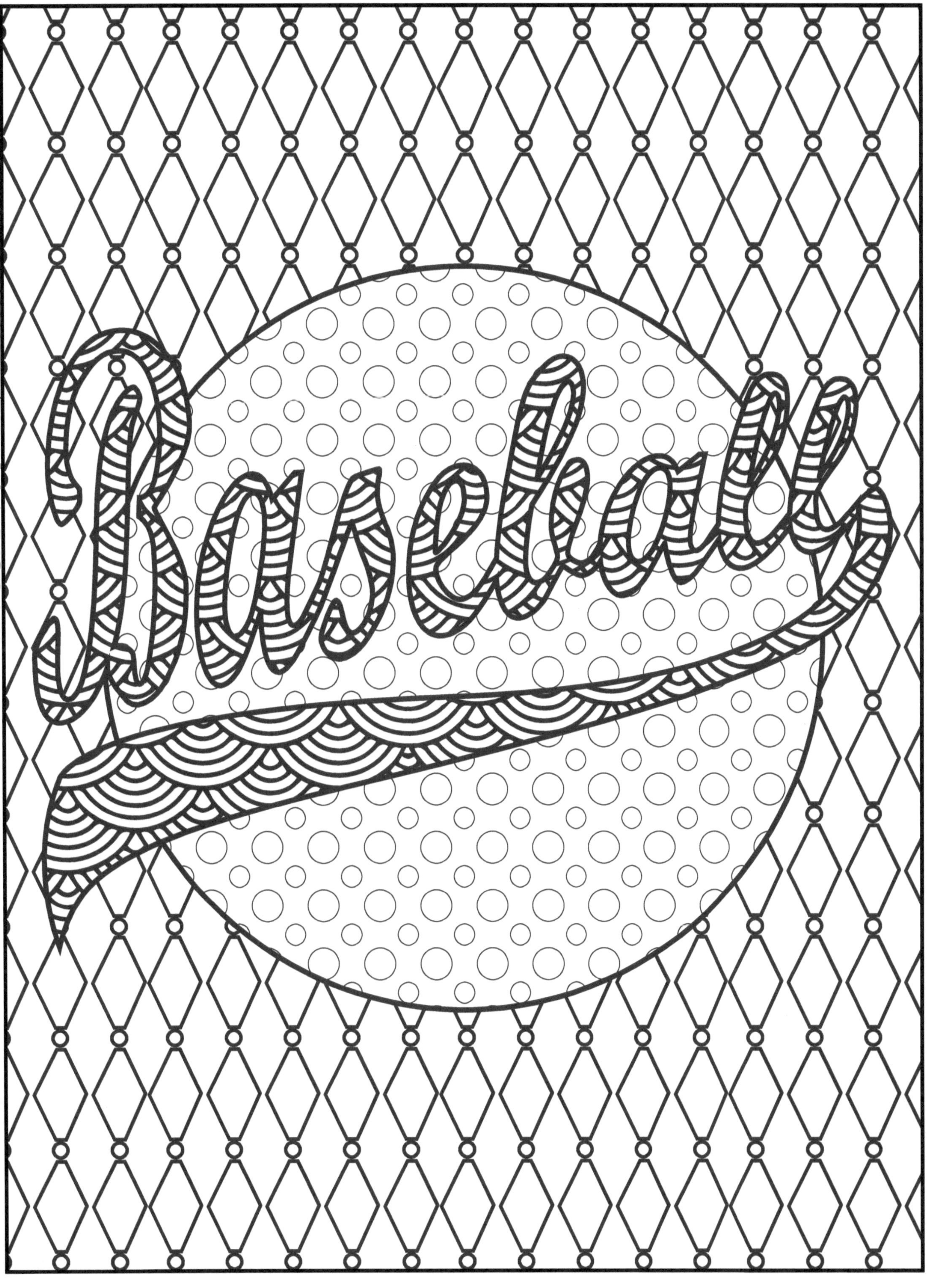
Baseball

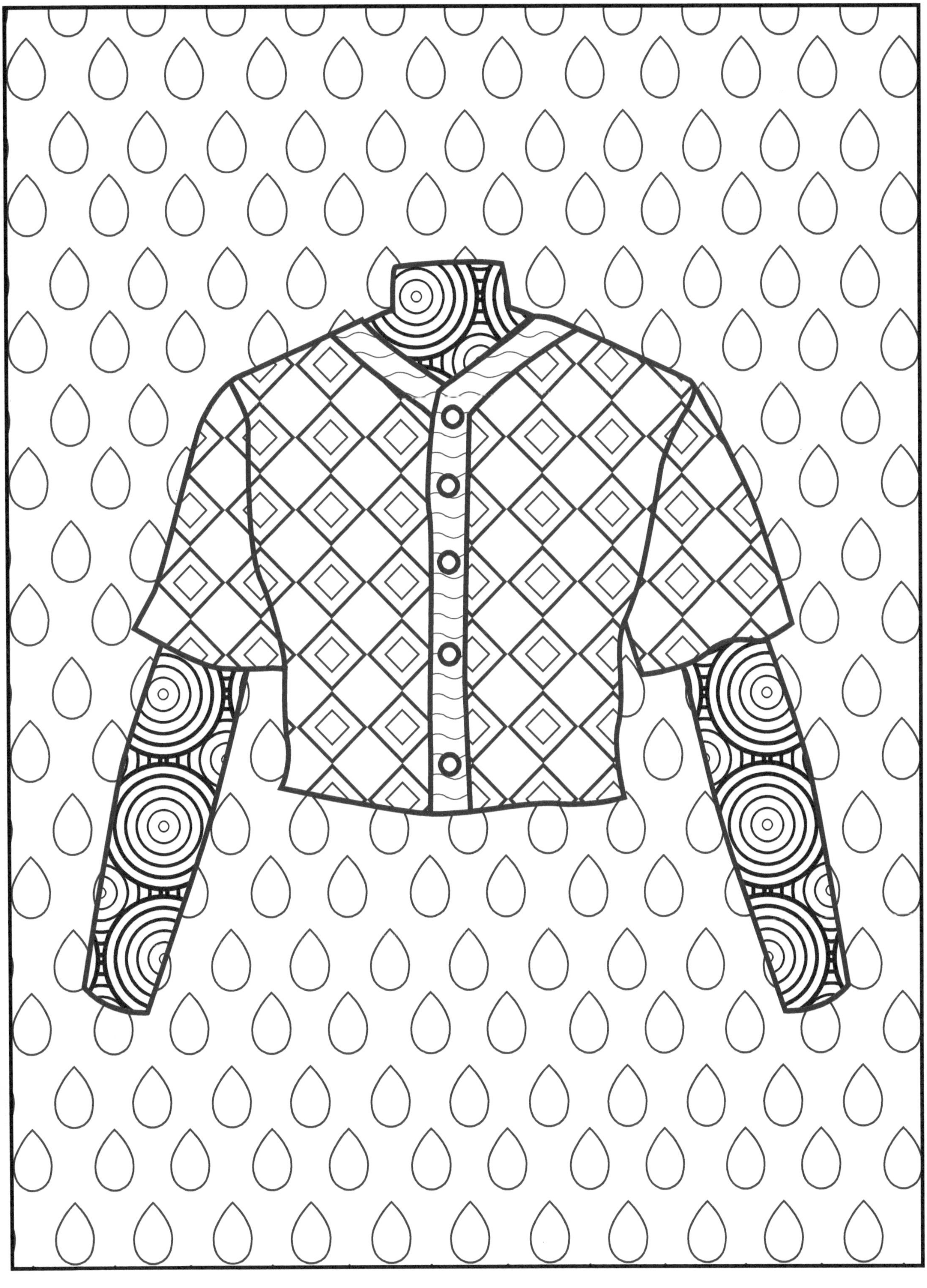

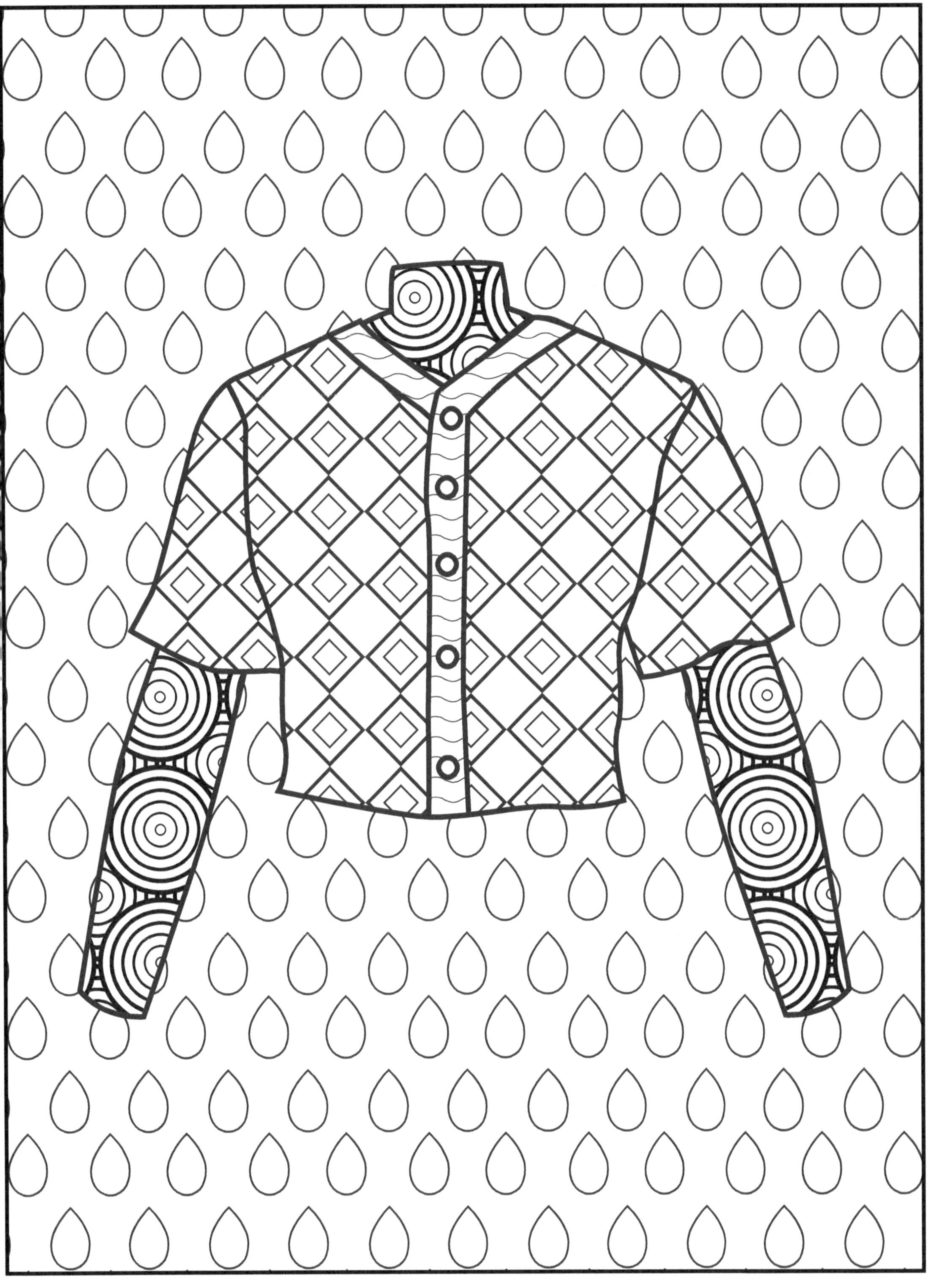

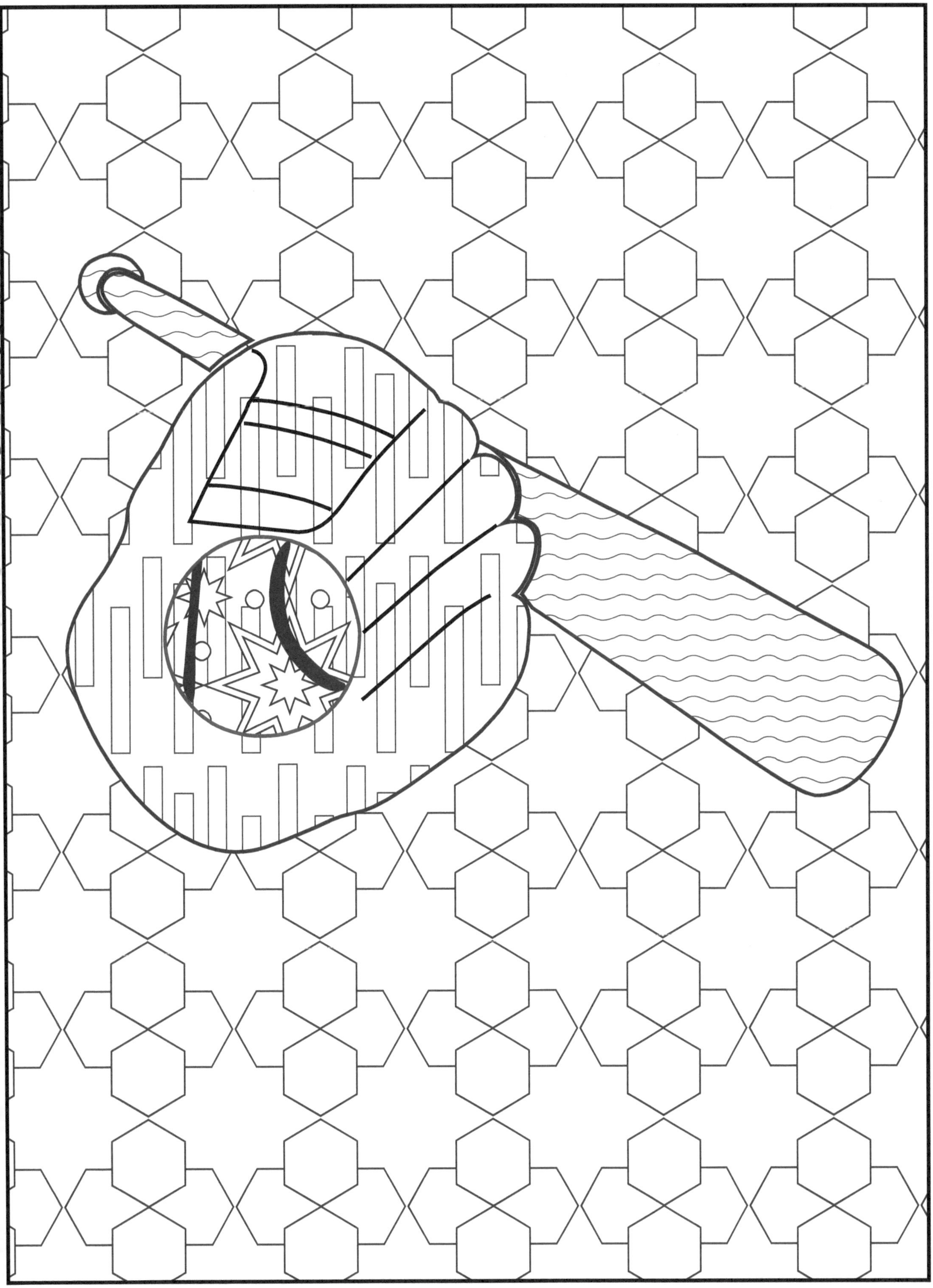

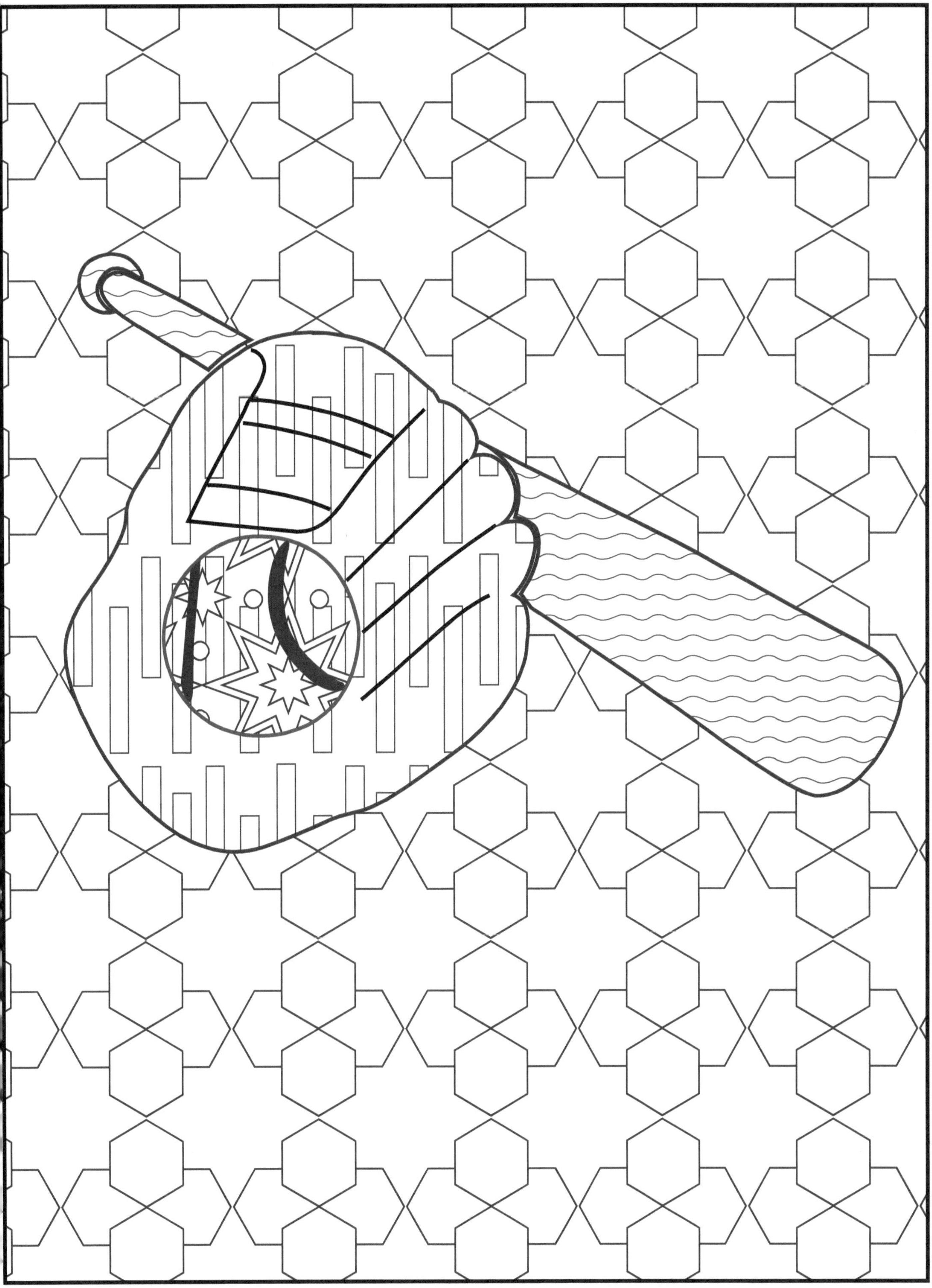

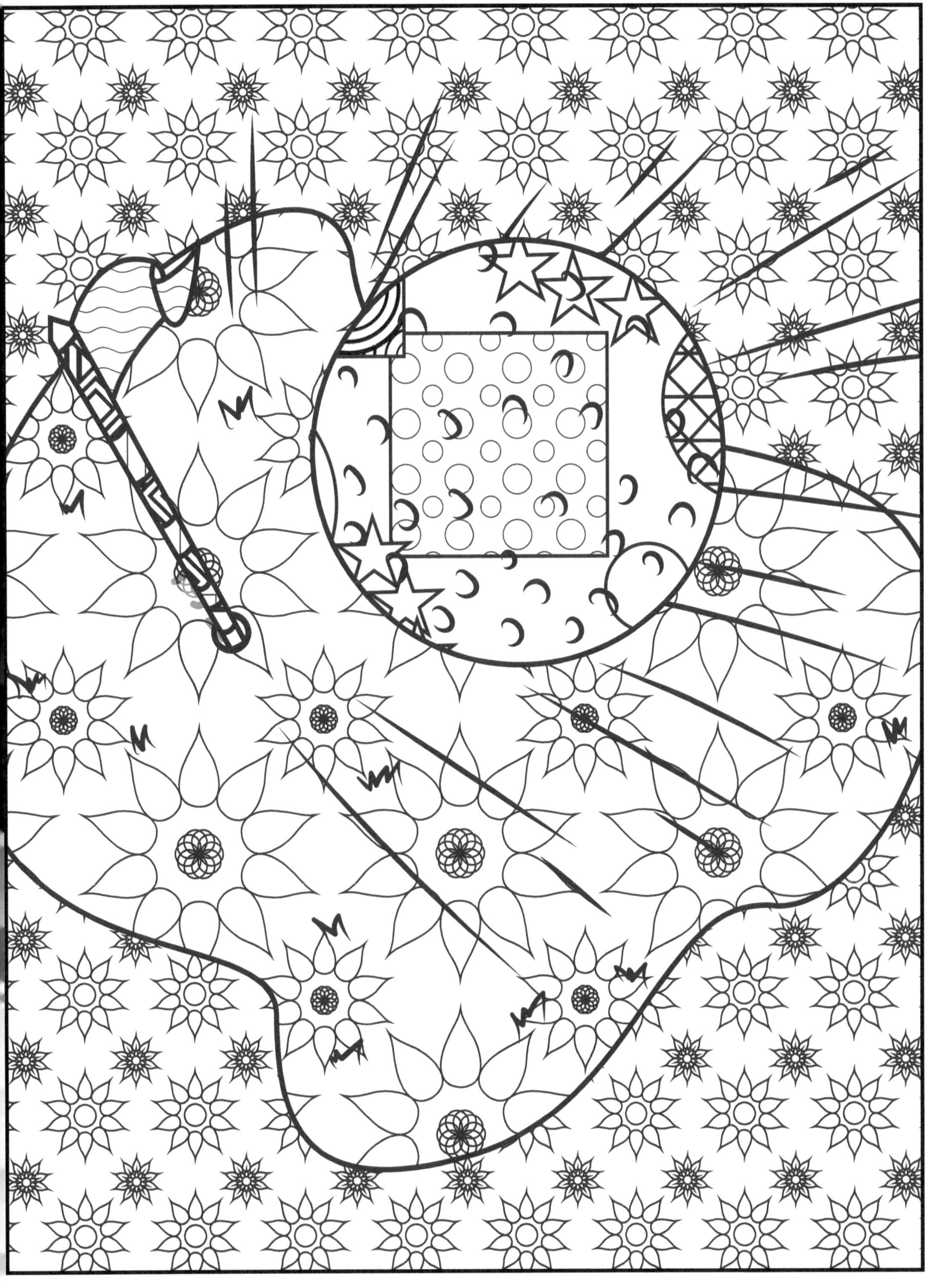

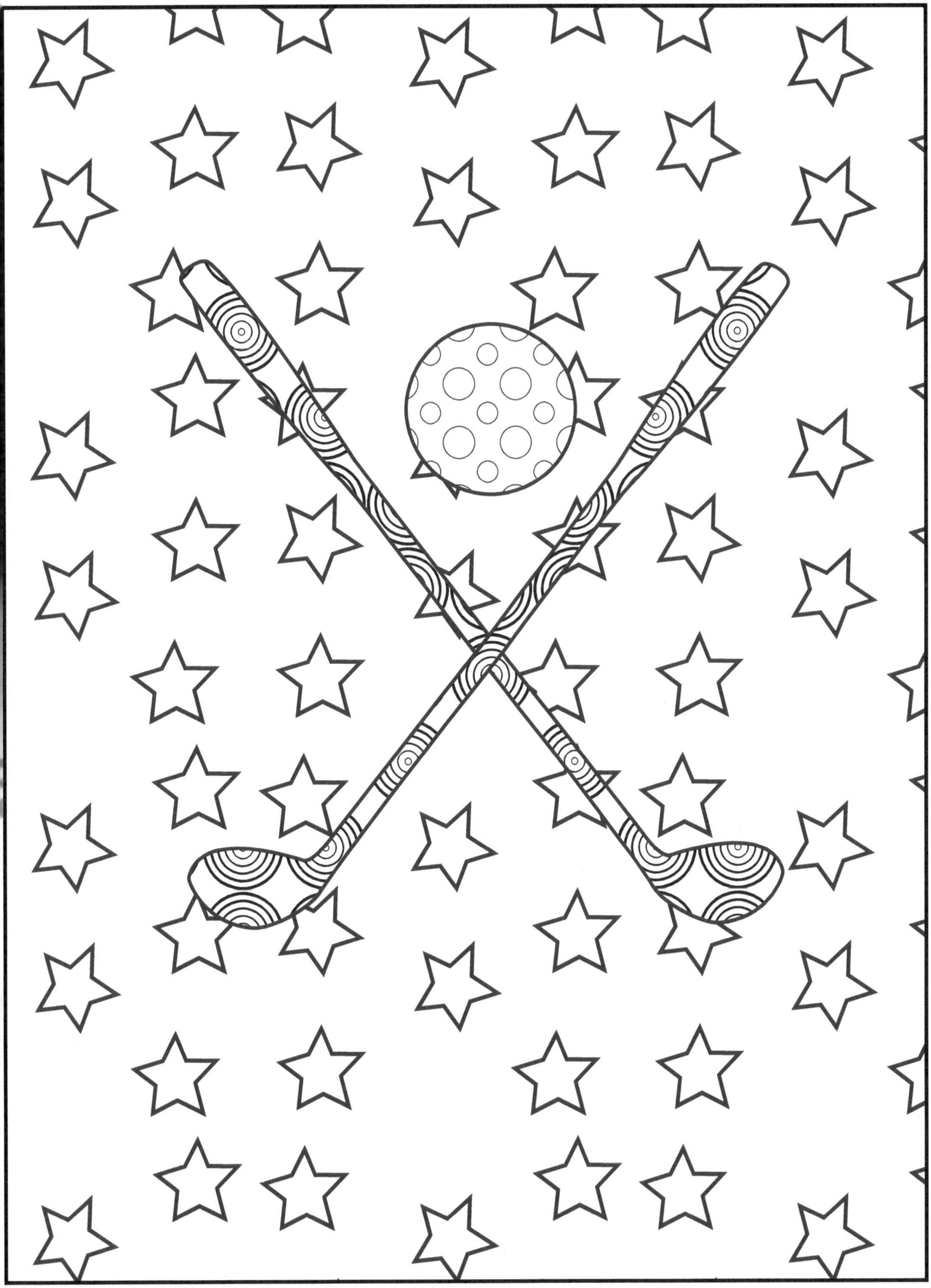

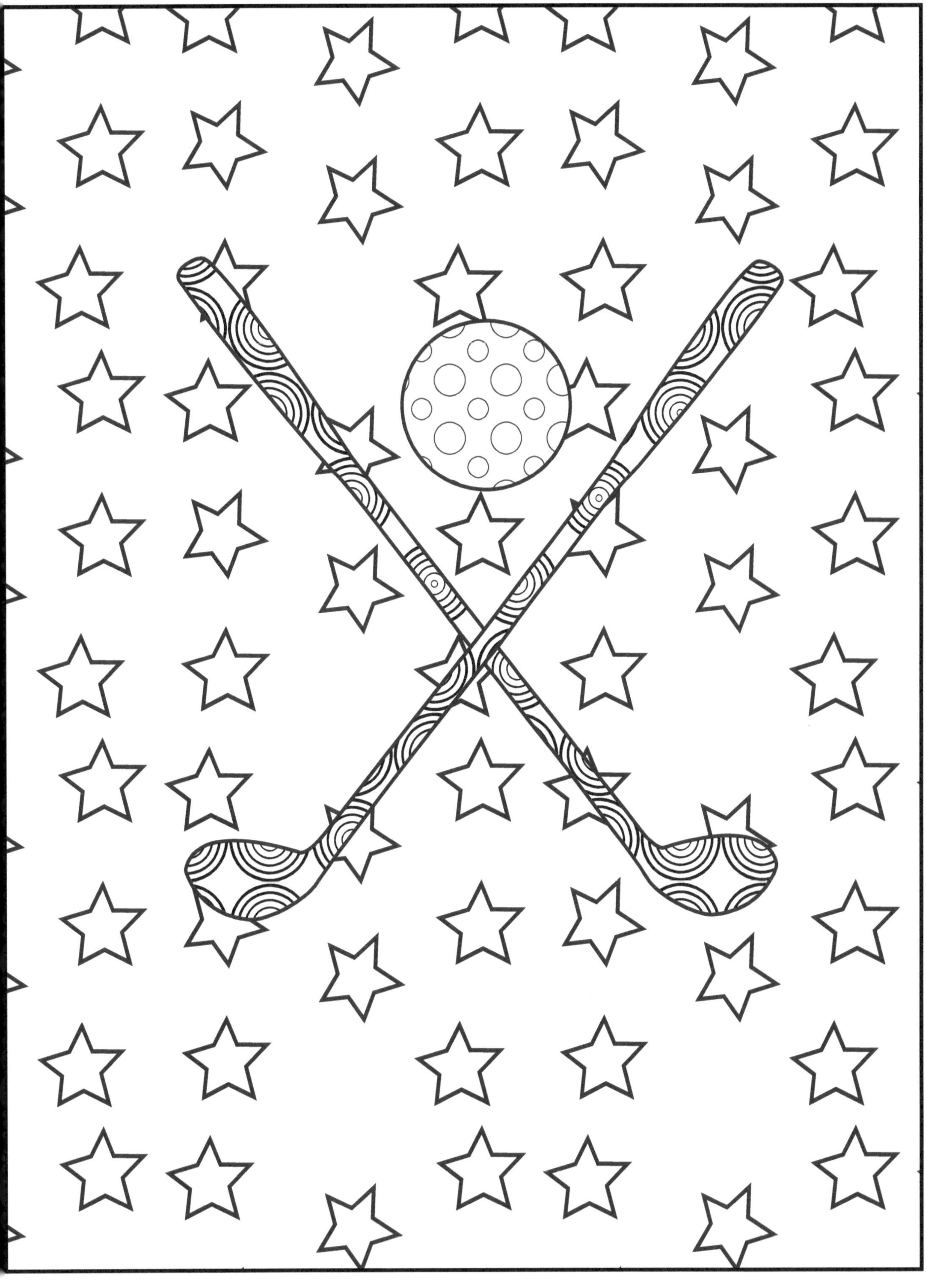

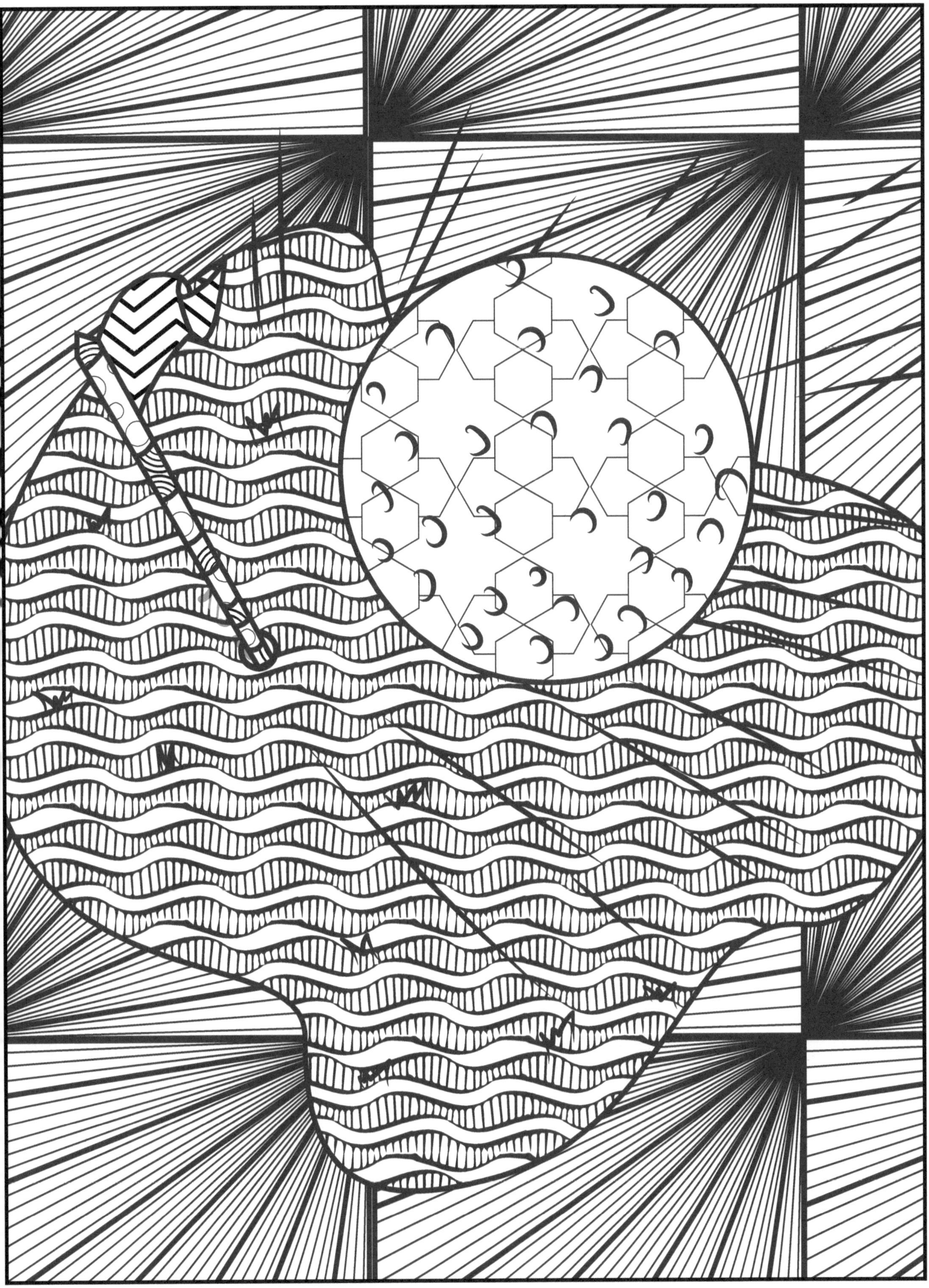

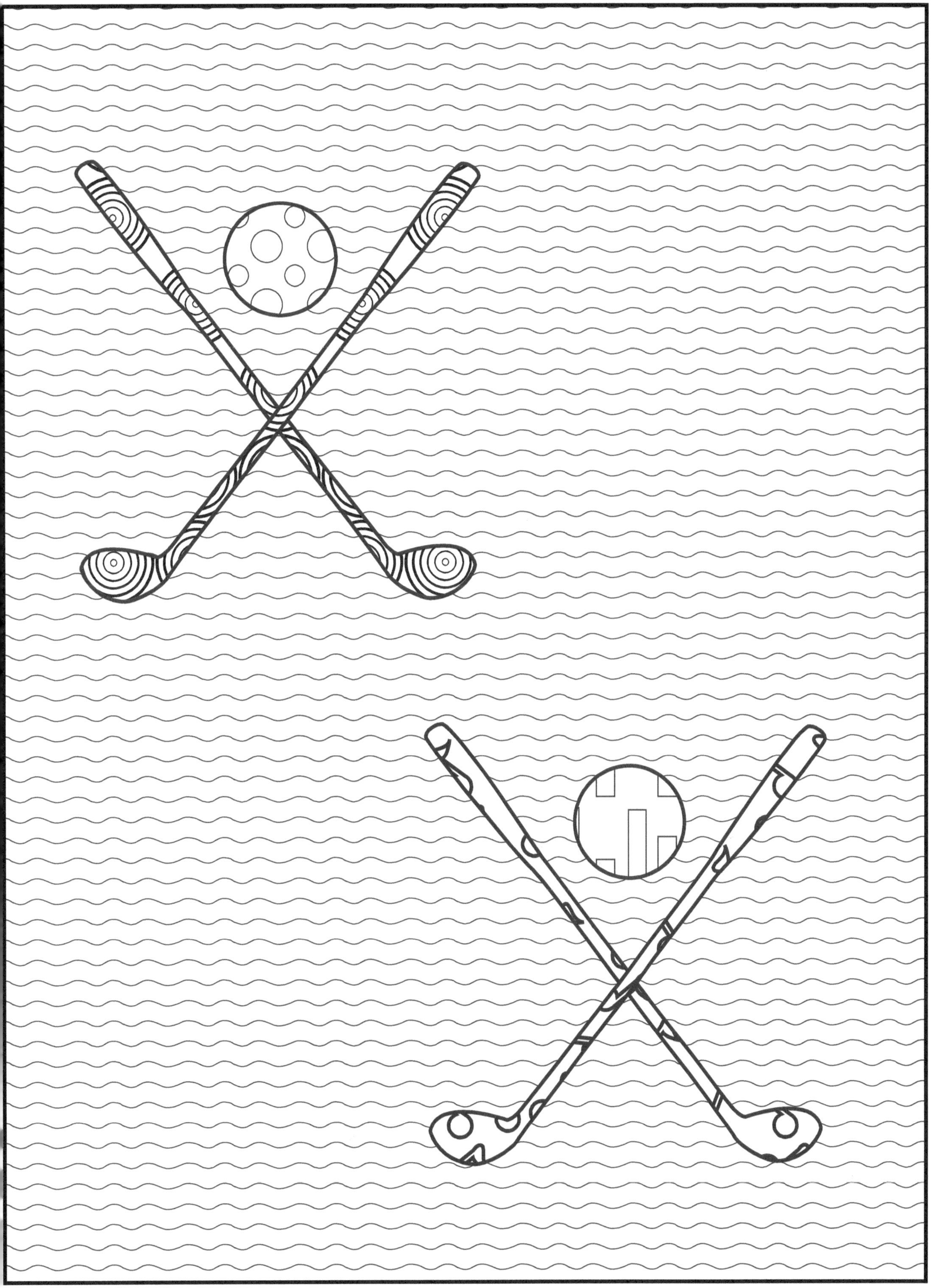

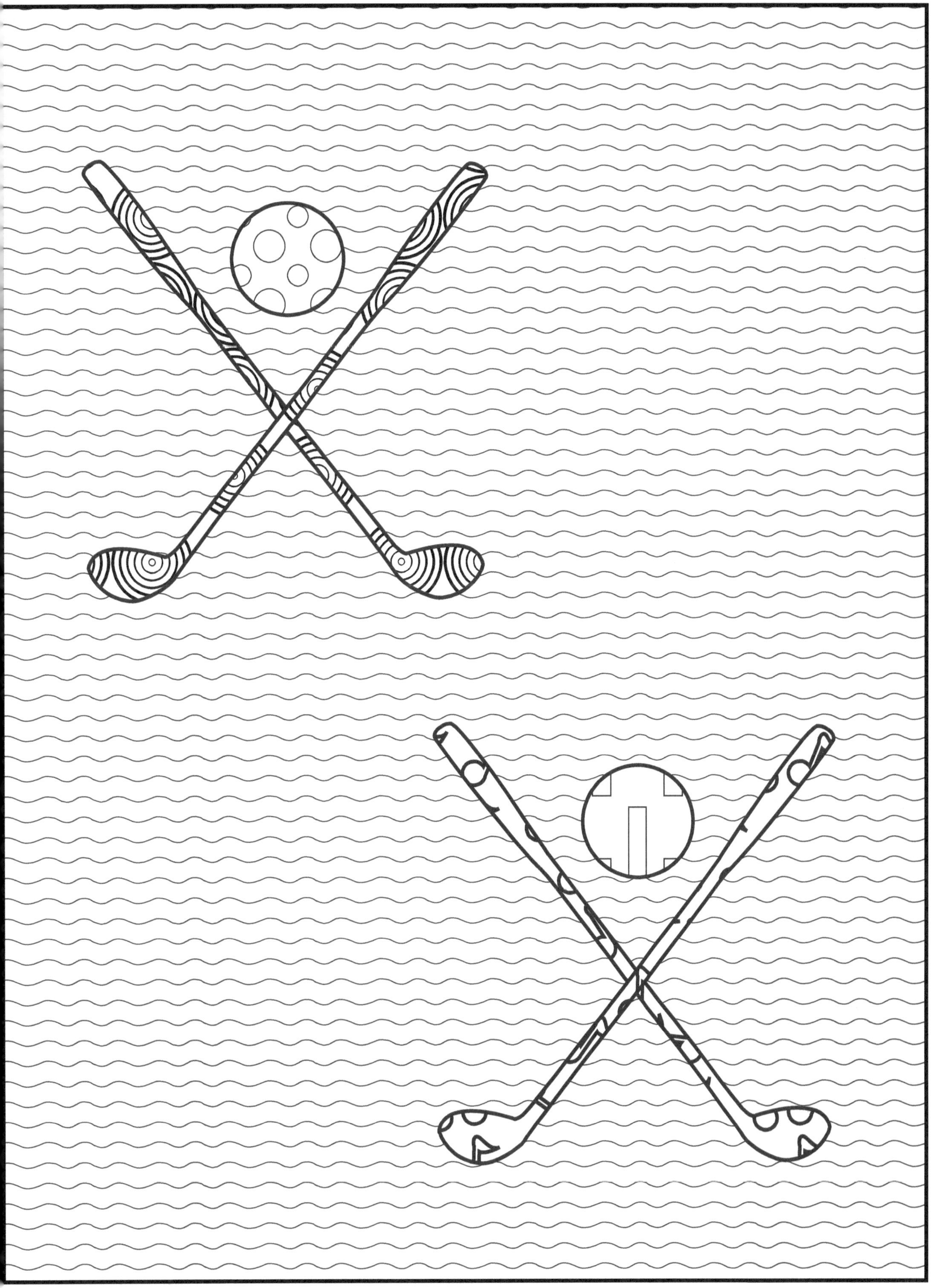

Made in United States
Troutdale, OR
02/26/2024

17988251R00071